Sm

MW00881528

How to Talk to People, Start Conversations, Improve Your Charisma, Social Skills and Lessen Social Anxiety

By Aston Sanderson

Small Talk by Aston Sanderson. Published by Walnut Publishing Company, Hanover Park, IL 60133

www.walnutpublishing.wordpress.com

Table of Contents

Introduction:
Why Small Talk Matters

Thank you for taking the time to download this book. You've taken the first step toward becoming an interesting conversationalist and someone that new people that you meet will remember.

Meeting new people can be hard for anyone, but with these proven strategies and tips, you'll find yourself growing more confident and beginning to enjoy the challenge of meeting someone new and developing a real, personal connection with them.

In these chapters, you'll learn how to increase your social skills and lessen your social anxiety.

At the completion of our 15-minute guide, you will have all the tools you need to get out and meet new people immediately with greater ease and confidence.

Once again, thanks for downloading this small talk guide, and I hope you find it to be helpful.

Why Is Small Talk Important?

Humans are, in our very essence, social animals.

We seek approval from others, and feel most comfortable fitting in with our families, our peers, our culture and the world at large.

Being socially inept can mean being rejected, which evolution has taught us is a bad feeling we'd like to avoid. Societies have been based for thousands of years on people getting along, working together, and marching together toward progress.

"Wow — all that, just from talking about the weather?" is what you might be thinking.

But it's true! We are social animals, and taking is our way of getting to know one another. Small talk is a way for people to break down their barriers and show each other through small conversation that the situation and the person they are talking to is safe. Only after establishing the tiniest bit of trust can we begin to form actual relationships through deeper conversation with those we don't know.

For anyone, meeting a stranger can be hard. But you don't need to hide away from fear of feeling nervous or having social anxiety.

Even for the most experienced, gregarious conversationalists, meeting new people always comes with the risk of rejection. But in these chapters you will learn how to conquer your fear, master your body language, find good topics to talk about and finally get out there and start meeting people with greater ease than before.

Chapter 1:
Mindset & Approach

Like anything in life, the most important thing about small talk is the way you approach it.

All the strategies, tips, hacks and conversation starters won't make a difference if you're stuck in a negative pattern of thinking. Don't get stuck in a fixed mindset based in fear, self-doubt or irrationality.

What is a fixed mindset? A fixed mindset means you think that who you are at this moment is who you have always been and who you will always be.

You may think:

"I'm not good at meeting new people."

"I always say the wrong thing and make a bad first impression."

"Social skills are just not my thing."

"I'm happy just staying home; they won't miss me at the party."

But those are all fixed mindset phrases.

You should focus on a growth mindset. A growth mindset means that you realize and accept that things are constantly changing in your life, all around you, and in your skills and actions.

You may not be the best conversationalist today, but everyone can get some strategies (like you've done by buying this book), practice them, and become better over time.

So let's turn those fixed mindset phrases into growth mindset phrases:

"I'm not good at meeting new people" becomes "I'm getting better at meeting new people."

"I always say the wrong thing and make a bad first impression" becomes "I am learning what to say around people, and improving the first impressions I make."

"Social skills are just not my thing" becomes "Social skills are an area of my life I have the capacity, ability and desire to improve."

"I'm happy just staying home; they won't miss me at the party" becomes "I am discovering new things about myself by getting out of my comfort zone, and I may be surprised how much fun I can have at a party."

See how the "I am only this way," types of thoughts became "I am becoming better and constantly improving and working on it" thoughts?

So, even if you think you are not the most beautiful social butterfly out there, you can remember that (to use a well-worn metaphor), all butterflies were once caterpillars.

If you believe that you are bad at social situations, you have already sabotaged yourself.

Believe that you can get better, and you've already taken the first, and possibly most difficult, step.

Chapter 2:
Nerves & How to Calm Them

We cross the threshold into the party. We deliver the wine we brought, hug the host, smile, and excitedly catch up with her.

But then — the host has dozens of other guests to attend to. She disappears as the doorbell rings.

Now what do we do?

The party seems full of people who are frightening to approach — people who *may* not like us. It's certainly a possibility.

We imagine walking up to someone and starting a conversation, but we wonder, will they like us? What will they think of us? Facing rejection is tough, no matter how small it is. Even if someone we don't know at all rejects us, we wonder why and may go down a spiral in our head of thinking why and getting down on ourselves.

Facing all that overthinking, when a party is just supposed to be fun, can be hard!

So how can we overcome nerves?

Breathe

It sounds simple, but when we are nervous, our bodies can take over without us realizing it. We may start to sweat, our breathing becomes rapid and shallow, our thoughts race, and our stomach can feel upset.

But what caused this physical reaction? Just our thoughts. So it works in reverse, too. Calming our bodies can also help to calm our minds, just as our minds affect our bodies.

So re-enter your body. Become aware that you are just standing in a room with people, not on the savannah about to be eaten by a lion. You are safe. Remember to breathe.

Focus on your breath, and your body will calm. Your heart rate will slow, your breathing will be more even, your stomach will settle, and your thoughts may stop racing.

Remember That Your Reaction is Normal

The no. 1 fear of many people is public speaking, as it's so ingrained in our biology.

And even the most practiced public speakers still get nervous before going on stage, often experiencing the bodily symptoms we just discussed.

No matter how confident you are, you can still feel nervous.

So remember that you are not the only person at the party, or the meeting, or work event who is feeling nervous.

If you remember this, you won't feel so alone. It's OK to admit to yourself that you are scared. Just remember that a lot of other people are, too.

Meet A Lot of New People

In psychology, when someone is afraid of spiders, a tactic used to help them get over that fear is called "systematic desensitization."

This means exposing the person over and over to spiders. First, it may just be a photo of spider. Then, it is larger photos of spiders. Then the psychologist holding a spider at a distance. Finally, the patient may be able, by him or herself, to hold the spider, and he or she has conquered the fear.

You can use the theory of systematic desensitization in your life as well, for meeting new people.

If you get used to meeting new people all the time, you will slowly become less frightened of it, just like the person with a fear of spiders.

So remember that at first, meeting new people will feel difficult and scary. But with each subsequent social situation, you will feel more and more comfortable.

Chapter 3:
Good Listening is Your Greatest Ally

It may sound weird to say that the best way to improve your conversational and small talk skills is to *say nothing at all*.

But that's exactly what this chapter is about.

Often, when we are engaged in a conversation that puts us out of comfort zone, we focus so much on saying the right thing and our minds racing that we forget to ever listen to what the other person is saying.

This may be comforting, to realize that a lot of people you talk to may not even be listening to what you say. But what kind of world is that, if we all go around talking and talking and never listening?

We can all work to become better listeners and engage each other on a deeper level.

Being a good listener is *extremely hard*. But just like the actual talking part of the conversation, it gets better with practice.

Here are three ways you can improve your listening:

Picture It

When you listen to someone else, it is easy to get wrapped up in thinking about your own experiences and how they relate. This a great strategy to converse with someone new, as shared experiences or having things in common is a great way to break down barriers.

But if the person begins sharing the details of their recent trip to the coast, and you immediately start imaging your most recent beach trip and thinking about what you can share about it, you are totally missing what the other person is saying.

So when they talk about the sailing adventure they want on, try to follow along by imaging it in your head. Can you picture the boat they took? When they gloss over that it was a three-day trip, you now can picture them sleeping on the boat each night. But wait — sleeping on the boat, was that hard? You know how it feels to get motion sickness in a car.

Now you have a great follow-up question. Maybe they actually found it really peaceful to sleep on the boat, like being rocked to sleep. Maybe they kept having nightmares it was sinking.

Really listening opens up limitless paths to go down in your conversation, and the only way to find those paths is to really listen for the details of someone's experience.

If you can imagine it yourself, you will probably ask yourself the same questions that person did while experiencing it.

So use your imagination to your advantage! Keep your brain busy focusing on the pictured experiences of the other person, instead of your own experience and what you will say about it.

Give Your Full Attention

It may sound obvious, but don't get distracted. Resist the urge to pull out your smartphone, even if it's just to look something up to share with the person, because your brain will immediately jump to thinking about all the notifications from social media or your unread emails you can see.

So remain fully engaged and present with the person you are speaking to.

Keep eye contact, and don't let your gaze wander around the party, event or restaurant, wherever you may be. This body language signals that you are bored or looking for an out of the conversation, so remain focused.

Imagine You'll Tell Someone Later

One of the best tricks for comprehending something and remembering it is thinking of explaining it to someone else.

This is a strategy that students can use for tests, but it's also a mind frame you can use when listening to someone else speak.

If you imagine you will tell someone later about the conversation, you will be more likely to pay attention and remember the important parts.

Chapter 4:
What to Say

Ugh, not the weather again!

Small talk gets a bad rap. Many people don't have particularly fascinating or important opinions or observations about the weather, and they don't want to hear anyone else's. They don't care about the local sports team. They don't want to talk about where they work, and for how long, again.

But remember that small talk plays an important social function in our society. This seemingly meaningless banter provides a way for us to get to know each other, and is a way for us to engage with each other that is non-threatening. Have you ever been having a bad day, and just the act of a cashier mentioning that the feel-better ice cream you bought yourself is their favorite flavor, too?

Even if it just makes you feel a tad better, interacting with people can help you feel not so wrapped up in your own thoughts, even if it is just "small" talk.

Small talk provides a low barrier of entry so we can all approach and talk to each other. If you walked up to strangers and asked them, "What is the most important memory from childhood?" you'd be pretty off-putting, to say the least.

But this is a question we'd feel comfortable discussing with best friends, our partners, or close family. At one time, each of those people was a stranger, too. And that wasn't the first thing we said to them.

So realize that anyone you speak to could become one of your close friends. It just doesn't happen overnight, or in the span on one conversation. Be patient, and make yourself and them comfortable at first by sticking to easy topics.

It can still be fun to talk about topics that aren't threatening or very deep.

You can try:

- Travel
- The host you both know
- Movies or TV you find you have in common
- The city you live in
- What you are doing for a coming holiday, or what you did for one that just passed

People love to talk about themselves, so if you can get someone to talk about themselves, instead of the weather, it will probably already be much more engaging for both of you.

Small talk doesn't have to be small! We'll show you how to have better small talk conversations, ones that actually lead to getting to know someone, in the next chapter.

But first, here are some ideas of what to say when engaged in small talk:

Comment on the Immediate Situation and Surroundings

If you are at a party and mention the good music, or the great snack table, or how great the turnout is, and the stranger you mention it to says more than one word, they are saying it's OK to engage them in conversation.

This is a great way to take something you have in common to test the waters with someone.

It's also immediately something you have in common, as you are at the same event. Maybe you both hate the current song that's playing, or maybe you both love it.

Just say something innocuous and see where it takes you.

Find Common Ground

Following off of the last tip, if you come across something you both have in common, more than the immediate situation or party you find yourselves at, make sure to explore that topic as much as you can! Maybe you both grew up playing soccer every summer. Maybe your grandmas are both from southern California. Maybe you both love dogs!

It could be anything, but sharing a common quality or passion with someone new instantly ingratiates us to them.

Give a Compliment

Everyone loves receiving a compliment. Don't go overboard, but you can comment on something small and simple.

Something like, "I love your shirt" is enough to get started chatting to someone new.

Always Give Information

Conversing is all about sharing. If you don't share, the other person will find it more difficult to bounce back to you in the conversation if you don't give them anything to go on.

If they ask you where you went to college, instead of just saying, "Iowa," you can say, "Iowa, it was a very small town, which I loved, because I grew up in a big city."

That's revealing something about yourself — that you grew up in a city but also enjoy living in a small town.

You could follow it up with, "Do you prefer the city? Have you spent any time in the country?" and now you have a conversation flowing!

If the person says, like our previous tip, something as small as, "Have you tried the popcorn at the snack table? It's so good."

Instead of just saying, "Yes, it's good." Or "No, I haven't," you can add, "Popcorn is basically the only reason I go to the movies, I've seen a lot of mediocre movies just to eat popcorn because movie theater popcorn is the best."

Now that person can agree or disagree with you, or ask you about a recent movie you've seen. They have a lot of options, since you've revealed something about yourself.

Stay Positive & Light

It's best not to start complaining or talking about something you don't like immediately after meeting someone new. No one likes to be around someone else who is super negative!

Also avoid the topics of health, religion and politics. These can be personal and controversial.

If the topic is heading toward something in one of these areas, you can steer it away.

If you are talking about (of course!) the weather, and the other person mentions the crazy storm that happens on election day, and asks you whether you went out in the storm to vote, you can say steer the conversation away from its political implications, and bring up a new topic instead of re-directing just to the weather, as that may give the other person an opportunity to bring up politics again.

Maybe say something like, "Oh yeah, I was out in that storm, I was worried about my dog all day! When I got home I couldn't find him, but eventually I found him hiding in the shower!"

Now you can safely talk about pets or dogs or fear of storms.

Chapter 5:
Not All Questions Are Created Equal

Questions, questions, questions!

Behind good listening, asking good follow-up questions is probably the most important part of mastering conversation and leveling up your small talk game.

So what makes a good question?

Good Questions Are Open-Ended

Don't just ask questions that can be answered with a "yes" or a "no." These sorts of questions are a conversation killer.

If you ask open-ended questions, you will get longer responses.

Remember the questions words: How, what, who, when, where and why.

As you are getting to know someone in your conversation and feeling more comfortable, breaking out "why" is a great strategy to use to probe a bit deeper.

If someone mentions that Bucelli's is their new favorite restaurant in town, you can ask them why, and then they have a chance to share more about something they are excited about and feel very positively toward.

Good Questions Are Superlative

"Superlative" refers to the extremes of something: The best, the most, the least, the craziest, someone's favorite.

When you ask a follow-up question, asking a superlative is a good way to have someone talk about something that they find engaging.

If someone mentions that they've been living in the same neighborhood for 10 years, you can ask them what the best thing about living there is, or their favorite thing about it. Clearly, they've stayed a while!

Don't Interrogate

Remember, don't let the other person do all the talking!

If you are feeling nervous, you may be inclined to share less instead of more. But then you give you conversational partner less to work with and ask you follow-up questions about.

So don't only ask questions, and don't ask a ton in rapid succession if you are not getting good responses back. This may be a sign that they are not interested in being asked so many questions about the topic you are inquiring about.

So also share about yourself for a bit, and feel comfortable doing it. If someone is sharing details about themselves with you, you should do the same as a courtesy with them.

Chapter 6:
Feedback and Ending a Conversation

Listen, you are not going to be the new best friend and Most Interesting Person everyone has ever met, and that's true for everyone at all times.

Having a fabulous connection with someone the first time you meet them is rare, and you should appreciate it when it happens.

But in a lot of cases, friendships or even acquaintances are built up over time through repeated meeting, shared experience, and many conversations, not just one or two.

So if you are speaking to someone and they are ready to leave the conversation, they may try to let you know in a subtle way, as most people do when engaged in small talk.

(And remember that someone leaving a conversation doesn't mean that it was bad. Maybe the other person is in a hurry or needs to speak to someone else at the work function to ensure they get that promotion they were hoping for. Maybe they want to catch up with someone they haven't seen in months who is also at the party. You don't know the reason someone is done talking to you, but it often is not just that you are not worth talking to.)

Here are some cues that someone is ready to end a conversation:

- They are not making eye contact, but constantly looking around

- They say "It was nice to meet you" or "It was nice talking to you," signaling that the conversation is over

- Their body language is "closed." This could be crossed arms, or their body pointing away from you and the conversation
- They mention another friend at the party and that they'd like to introduce the two of you, this person will probably not join that conversation

It's also nice to give someone an out of a conversation. If you have only been talking to that person for a long time at an event with a lot of people, you both should meet more than each other.

You can say something like:

- "Well, I'm sure you have a lot of other people to catch up with"
- "It's been so great talking to you, but I'm going to mingle a bit"
- "It's been great to talk to you, but I think I should meet a few of our hosts other friends, too"

Chapter 7:
Conversation Starters: A List

At a loss for topics to talk about, ways to approach someone, or how to keep the conversation going after it's stalled a bit?

Use some of these suggestions:

- Have you always done this [profession], or have you worked as anything else?

- If you could fly anywhere in the world at no cost tomorrow, where would you go?

- What was the best job you had growing up?

- What's the best advice you've ever gotten?

- What's the strangest compliment someone has given to you?

- Do you have a book, movie or TV show that you love, but everyone else hates? What about something everyone else loves, but you hate?

- If you could only eat one food for the rest of your life, what would you choose?

- Does your family have any recipes that have been passed down for generations, or that are secret?

- What was the last travel experience you had?

- What's your favorite thing to do on the weekends?

- Have you ever lived anywhere else? How is this place different?

- Do you have a hidden talent, or a surprising hobby?

- What's your favorite app on your phone?
- Have you read any good books recently?
- Have you ever had a boss who asked you to do something crazy?
- What's your favorite unknown restaurant?
- If you could have any superpower, what would it be?
- What would you teach a college course on, if you could?
- If you could have any animal as a pet, what one would you choose?

Chapter 8:
Body Language

We say a lot with our bodies, and we read a lot about how other people are feeling based on their body language, even if we don't realize we are all constantly communicating with this secret language.

So you need to make sure that your body language is saying what you want it to. Your body will probably naturally show how you are feeling, so if you are interested in speaking to someone, you will show it.

However, if you are not really interested in speaking to someone, or you are feeling nervous, your body may be sending the wrong signals to the other person.

Your body should be "open." That means no crossed arms, cross legs if you are sitting, or turning your body angled away from the person you are talking to.

Other tips:

- Smile and appear friendly
- Make eye contact
- Stand a comfortable distance away from someone, not too close, nor sitting too close if one a couch
- Avoid using your phone during the conversation
- Avoid touching your face or hair excessively or do other nervous habits like picking at your nails
- Don't tap your foot, as it could appear that you are impatient to leave the conversation

Chapter 10:
Why You'll Make a Mistake and Why It Doesn't Matter

None of us is perfect. Even the greatest communicators, most gregarious people and biggest and most beautifully-winged social butterflies stumbles sometimes in a social situation. Maybe your conversation partner isn't making it easy for you and you have to do all the work. Maybe you had a bad day at the office and your mind is still at work. Maybe you are just having an off day or misjudged a joke that you thought would be funny and therefore misjudged the situation. That's all totally ok!

We all make mistakes, and rest assured that everyone thinks about themselves a lot more than they ever think about you. Try to think of your most embarrassing moment from grade school or middle school. You can remember it pretty vividly, can't you? Did it happen in front of a lot of people? How many of your classmates do you think remember it today? Can you think of embarrassing moments of others you witnessed in school? Probably not as many as you can think of for yourself.

So remember to relax, it will all be ok. It feels overwhelming and terrible in the moment, but no one will remember your embarrassing social faux pas.

Another thing to remember about social skills is that they are learned. No one is born a social communicator. We all have to grow up and learn language and the ways people interact in our specific culture. If being gregarious and popular were innate, people would be revered across cultures. But it can be hard to talk to someone who doesn't share the same social rules and conversation markers from another country.

Some people are predisposed to liking social interaction more, or have had more experience or are more naturally inclined to it. But they are just social clues that can be learned, so you can learn them to.

Your social skills are a muscle, and just like when you are weight training, you need to stretch them, work them, and keep stretching and working them and challenging them to ever grow those muscles. Now, you may feel like you are lifting very little in our weight lifting metaphor.

Maybe you can only pick up the bar. But after you go through these strategies and start to learn more about social skills, you will definitely make some missteps. And that's OK! It just means you are improving. As long as you learn from the situation, realize what you could have done better and then move on.

Your social skill and small talk muscles are growing with each interaction, and especially those that you feel you didn't totally crush. Don't freak out and go into a downward spiral thinking that you are bad at small talk. You are growing, little caterpillar and future social butterfly, and that's what important.

Conclusion:
Time to Use What You've Learned

Thanks again for taking the time to download this book on small talk, I hope that you've gained strategies you can use right now to improve your social skills and lessen social anxiety.

Remember, you can get out there today and use what you've learned. Remember these general tips:

- Be confident and have a growth mindset

- Accept that you will feel nervous and that is normal

- Use the surroundings to start conversations

- Ask open-ended questions

- Share about yourself; don't give short answers

- Have friendly and open body language

- Avoid controversial topics

- Let the other person politely end the conversation; or do it yourself

- Remember that when you feel you made a social flub, it means you are working your conversation muscles and getting better!

If you enjoyed this book, please take the time to leave me a review on Amazon. I appreciate your honest feedback, and it really helps me to continue producing high quality books.

Further Reading

Like what you read? Read more in our non-fiction how-to series, coming soon.

What do you want to learn? Give us feedback, ideas, or just say hi at walnutpublishing@gmail.com.

40434486R00018

Made in the USA
Middletown, DE
12 February 2017